Original title:
The Touch of Velvet

Copyright © 2025 Creative Arts Management OÜ
All rights reserved.

Author: Jameson Hartfield
ISBN HARDBACK: 978-1-80586-037-2
ISBN PAPERBACK: 978-1-80586-509-4

Whispers of a Softer World

In a land where cushions reign,
Pillows float in joyous strain,
Silken dreams and laughter dance,
Tickled toes in a soft romance.

Cats in capes, oh what a sight,
Balancing atop the night,
With a purr that cracks the air,
Like jokes slipped from a fluffy chair.

Feathered hats on snoring bears,
Mirth spills out from comfy lairs,
Each chuckle cradled in a fold,
Silly secrets softly told.

Socks that giggle when they play,
On a rainy, lazy day,
Join the prance of comfy cheer,
As laughter wraps us, far and near.

The Embrace of Sensuous Night

In the light of the moon so bright,
Cats plot mischief, oh what a sight!
They jump and tumble with grace,
Landing softly, not leaving a trace.

A dance on the edge of a quilted bed,
Dreams of fish swim in their head.
If only they'd share their crafty schemes,
Instead, they just nap, lost in dreams.

Whispers Among Lush Draperies

Behind the curtains, secrets are spun,
The couch cushions hide laughter and fun.
A tickle, a nudge, oh what a game,
Pillow fort castles, who's to blame?

Tangled in blankets, limbs all a mess,
Witty remarks, who'll wear the stress?
A soft cozy world, where chaos thrives,
As we giggle like children, feeling so alive.

The Gentle Art of Fondness

Hugs that are bouncy, not quite sincere,
A laugh when you stumble, it's all in good cheer.
With cuddly cushions and giggly glee,
Laughter hangs thick, like honey from a tree.

Pats on the back, a gentle embrace,
But when you trip, oh what a disgrace!
Fond memories linger, wrapped up so tight,
In the fabric of love, on this silly night.

Threads of Enchantment

Crafty creations from yarn and delight,
Stitching together a cozy night.
Beware the sharp needles, oh what a fright,
For just one poke, and it's tears in sight!

The magic of threads that dance and play,
A patchwork of laughter that brightens the day.
Quirky designs, what fun we'll weave,
In the fabric of folly, just let's believe!

Touching the Ethereal

In dreams, we dance with fluffy socks,
Like clouds that graze the ticklish rocks.
Ghosts of laughter swirl in the air,
We prance through giggles, without a care.

With every touch of fabric so rare,
A wink from fate, a playful stare.
We float, we glide on whims and threads,
As shadows chuckle, beneath our beds.

Silken Pathways Through Time

Down the hallway, we take a chance,
With satin slippers, we start to prance.
Each slide and glide just makes us grin,
In this stitched parade, let the fun begin.

Wobbling wildly, off-balance we swerve,
The floor beneath us starts to curve.
With laughter echoing through each room,
Time winks at us, dispelling gloom.

Hushed Murmurs in Tapestry

Under blankets, whispers take flight,
Secrets traded in the dimming light.
We giggle soft, like kittens at play,
In this woven world, we'll never stray.

With tickles hidden in corner seams,
We chase after the silliest dreams.
Every thread a tale, a cheeky jest,
In our own kingdom, we're truly blessed.

Shades of Comfort and Longing

Each snuggle wraps us like a spell,
We plot and scheme, oh do tell,
In moments soft, our worries untwine,
In this cozy realm, we sip on time.

We roll and tumble, cushions collide,
With every splat, we burst with pride.
Our little circus of chortles and squeals,
The finest performance, crafted with zeal.

The Quiet Linger of Warmth

A cushion on my couch so deep,
It swallows all my thoughts to sleep.
I dive headfirst, a cozy fall,
The laughter echoes through the hall.

The sun creeps in, a golden tease,
It tickles toes and warms the knees.
My cat's a king, a furry throne,
Who knew such joy could feel like bone?

The Caress of Gentle Raindrops

A tap dance on my windowpane,
Each drop a joke, a playful rain.
The puddles form a wobbly face,
As if the sky's in some wild race.

Umbrellas swirl like jellybeans,
The people laugh at all the scenes.
With galoshes on, I stomp around,
The world's my stage, the ground's my sound!

A Whisper Under Satin Skies

Stars above in twinkled array,
They wink at us, come out and play.
The moon's a smile, quite round and bright,
A cheeky grin, a beacon of light.

We dance beneath those shiny beams,
Sharing secrets, goofy dreams.
With every giggle, clouds go by,
Who knew the night could laugh and sigh?

Lush Textures of Forgotten Dreams

A blanket fort, my secret space,
Where all my worries lose their race.
I build my kingdom, soft and grand,
With cushions piled like grains of sand.

Stuffed creatures plot a silly scheme,
They whisper plans that make me beam.
In this cocoon, I reign with glee,
Life's quirks unfold so wonderfully!

The Allure of Silken Embers

In a room filled with fabric,
A cat plots with glee,
Pouncing on cushions,
As fluffy as can be.

Laughter erupts from a chair,
Whispers of mischief dance,
With threads all around,
Who knew silk had a chance?

A slip on the floor, oh dear!
Did someone just trip?
The couch erupts in giggles,
A fabric-loving trip!

Yet amid all the chaos,
A warmth starts to glow,
Wrapped in cheeky moments,
Where soft laughter flows.

Swaying Under Satin Skies

Under skies that glimmer,
A dance takes its place,
With satin slips and jubilance,
And a comical grace.

People twirl in pajamas,
With fringe and with flair,
While a cat steals the spotlight,
In a silky nightmare!

A moonlight invitation,
To flaunt what we got,
With buttons popping loudly,
In a bright polka dot.

So sway with those sparkles,
Let laughter be your guide,
For under these satin skies,
We giggle and slide!

Echoes of Warm Embraces

In the hum of a living room,
Where quilts gently reign,
Each cuddle a snicker,
And a laughter-filled strain.

With fluffs piled high,
And pillows that jest,
One jumps on the couch,
It's a velvet-clad fest!

Cups clink with delight,
As snacks scatter wide,
Oh dear, where's the cake?
It slipped, what a ride!

In these cozy embraces,
Where chaos meets cheer,
Life's brightest moments thrive,
With all that we hold dear.

A Veil of Night's Warmth

Stars twinkle and tease,
As the night wears a grin,
Amid blankets of laughter,
Let the fun times begin.

A rogue sock on the floor,
Takes a leap, quite absurd,
While echoes of giggles,
Twist and turn with a word.

With hot cocoa chuckles,
And marshmallows that fly,
The warmth of our banter,
Makes the evening's heart sigh.

Under shadows we hide,
But the joy shines so bright,
In this playful embrace,
Of warmth through the night.

Silken Paths of Serenity

In a world of fluff and flair,
Where pillows dance without a care.
Cats in coats of shimmery sheen,
Leave us laughing, oh what a scene!

On trails where softness reigns supreme,
Dogs in pajamas fulfill the dream.
Balloons float by, they giggle and squeak,
Life's little wonders, oh so unique!

With slippers that give a mocking sway,
Fuzzy creatures lead the way.
Whispers of joy in the lightest thread,
Tickle your toes until they dread!

So let's prance in a fabric delight,
Sewn with laughter, day and night.
In this realm of whimsical grace,
We twirl around in a warm embrace!

Cradled by Night's Gentle Hand

Stars in pajamas shine so bright,
As they giggle through the night.
Here comes the moon in a velvet cape,
Winking at dreams, a shape-shifting grape!

Cuddly bears throw a midnight bash,
In tea cups of dreams, they swirl and splash.
Pillow fights with a twist of delight,
Feathers abound, a chaotic sight!

Night's gentle hand begs us to stay,
As we roll in laughter, silly display.
With dreams that pop like bubbles of cream,
We ride on clouds, oh what a dream!

So let's hang on to this playful ride,
Through milky ways where joy can't hide.
A bedtime tale spun with soft glee,
In the arms of night, we're ever free!

A Tidal Wave of Caresses

Waves of giggles crash ashore,
Tickling toes in a silly roar.
Splashing puddles of laughter abound,
As soft whispers float all around.

Puppies in surfboards, riding high,
Wobbling together, oh my, oh my!
Each tumble brings a chuckle anew,
In this ocean of chaos, who knew?

Seagulls wear shades, so dapper and bright,
Cawing jokes at the fading light.
Jellyfish dance with a squishy flow,
Making fish laugh with their silly show!

So let's dive deep in this frothy foam,
And surf the giggles far from home.
In the sea of humor, let's all sway,
Riding the tides of joy today!

Dreamscapes in Svelte Shadows

In twilight's dance, where secrets creep,
Shadows play hide and seek, oh so deep.
Bouncing moonbeams toss and twirl,
Through the air, they spin and whirl.

Kittens plot in cozy corners,
Knitting dreams while the world warns us.
With a stitch of giggles and a purr or two,
They sew tales of night that seem brand new.

Night owls hoot a tune so groovy,
In feathered hats, they move so smooth-y.
Wobbling on tree branches, they chirp,
Making all awake with a silly burp!

So let's wander where shadows shimmer,
In this realm where laughter's a glimmer.
In the fabric of dreams, we'll clever play,
Until dawn wraps us in a bright new day!

Whispers of a Silken Embrace

A fabric's whisper here and there,
Can't quite tell if it's a chair.
Slippery slides in socks I wear,
Caught in a hug, I gasp for air.

A couch that softly grips my seat,
Where laundry and I laugh and meet.
It's like a date, but less discreet,
With cushions making me feel sweet.

The curtain sways with secret glee,
Is it just me, or joy's decree?
Laughter lingers, wild and free,
As I tumble, oh woe is me!

So here's to softness, what a play,
In cozy realms, I waste the day.
With every grin, I rue the fray,
While silly things come out to play.

Caress of Midnight Dreams

The night is young, the sheets parade,
In cotton dreams, I've wildly strayed.
I toss and turn, a grand charade,
With pillows plotting plans I made.

A blanket monster snugly bites,
I chuckle loud at midnight sights.
It cuddles tight, a playful fright,
As laughter echoes through the nights.

The quilt, it tickles, oh so sly,
Like feathered friends that flutter by.
In cozy realms, the stars comply,
As I invent new ways to fly.

These midnight tales, they dance and weave,
With every snicker, I believe.
What fun it is to moan and grieve,
For softness leads me to perceive!

Embracing the Soft Shadows

In corners dark, there lies a dream,
Of whispers wrapped in velvet seam.
A gentle rustle, oh what a theme,
I laugh aloud; it feels like cream.

The dust bunnies throw a party here,
They sway and twirl without a fear.
They tickle toes while I sit near,
In shadows soft, we shed a cheer.

A playful brush, the wall does tease,
With fuzzy edges, it aims to please.
I trip and giggle, oh what a breeze,
In this warm hug, I find my ease.

So let the shadows softly sway,
In gentle arms where fun may play.
I'll waltz with whispers, come what may,
As laughter grows, and worries fray.

Textures of a Gentle Caress

The carpet's fibers softly hum,
They know my feet, and here I come.
With every step, my joy's a drum,
A lighthearted jig, oh what fun!

My sofa grins, it holds me tight,
As cushions speak of pure delight.
I snuggle deep, no end in sight,
A fluffy kingdom, day turns night.

The curtains dance in playful jest,
With every breeze, they know me best.
I grin and wiggle, can't resist,
In textures soft, I find my rest.

So here I twirl in gentle bliss,
Each fabric's laugh, I can't dismiss.
In moments wrapped, how sweet it is,
To cherish cozy, silly kiss.

A Dance of Luxurious Light

In a gown of soft delight,
Twirls the cat in moonlit night.
With every spin, a feather flies,
Knocking over grandma's pies.

A squirrel winks from the nearby tree,
Chasing after a bumblebee.
"Oh dear, not my fancy hat!"
Said the man, who looked quite flat.

Beside him, a dog in silly glee,
Wears a scarf and dances free.
With every leap, he makes a show,
While the crowd erupts in joyful woe.

Laughter fills the air tonight,
Underneath the warm starlight.
With silly moves and fumbles galore,
They dance until their feet are sore.

Tapestries of Gentle Stillness

In a room where echoes creep,
Woolly blankets pile in heaps.
A puppy snuggled, fast asleep,
Dreams of chasing tails and sheep.

A corner hides a friendly chair,
Worn-out cushions, old but rare.
When one sits, it groans in glee,
As if to say, "Come laugh with me!"

The houseplants sway with gentle pride,
Whispering secrets of those who've cried.
Their leaves dance on a drafty breeze,
Tickling noses with such finesse.

In stillness, the grandfather clock,
Tells a joke with every tick-tock.
Time might pause for a while that day,
But laughter finds its sneaky way.

Shadows Shaped in Satin

In the corner where shadows play,
A turtle wears a shawl of gray.
He shuffles slowly, oh so grand,
Beside a snail with a fancy band.

A mouse in a vest joins the scene,
With tiny shoes, a living dream.
His laughter dances, oh so bright,
As he pirouettes in the twilight.

The walls giggle, with stories old,
Of fancy dreams in fabric bold.
A cat rolls by, a clumsy sight,
Unraveling yarn, oh what a plight!

Among shadows, secrets unspool,
Where laughter reigns and no one's cruel.
For in this world of silliness true,
Every misstep brings something new.

A Cloak of Warmest Memories

Beneath a pile of knitted joy,
A turtle's hiding, oh what a ploy!
With countless tales stitched in thread,
Of wild adventures long since fled.

A cat appears, with mischief brewed,
Pawing at tales in an attitude.
"Let's relive that time at the fair!"
She says with a purr and a ruffled hair.

A squirrel chimes in, "Oh, how we danced,
In colorful outfits, we were entranced!"
They chuckle with glances shared,
For memories last, and laughter is spared.

Wrapped in warmth, the moments glow,
With every laugh, a new tale flows.
In the cloak of camaraderie bright,
They dance and play through the night.

The Embrace of Night's Fabric

In shadows deep, where giggles dwell,
A fabric hugs like stories to tell.
Cloaked in whispers, the night does scheme,
Tickling dreams, like a silly dream.

The stars play tag in the velvet sky,
Where owls debate and kittens nigh.
With every rustle of the cloth so bright,
A chuckle echoes through the moonlit night.

The breeze takes a sip of the sweet night air,
While socks dance flamingo, quite unaware.
A tapestry woven of laughter and light,
Unfolding fun, in the quiet of night.

So when you drift on whispers of gray,
Remember the fabric, let laughter stay.
For in the dark, we find a spark,
In the embrace of a night quite a lark.

Midnight's Gentle Indulgence

In the deep of night, a treat to behold,
A cozy quilt wrapped, never feels cold.
Socks with stripes tell jokes all around,
In midnight's embrace, fun is unbound.

A dance of the pillows, a waltz on the floor,
Each snuggle invites a curious score.
The moon does giggle, the stars all snicker,
As our sleepy eyes wander, they just grow quicker.

With blankets like clouds cradling dreams,
Each chuckle weaves through the softest seams.
The night hums softly, a quirky tune,
While laughter slips gently, beneath the moon.

Nestled so snugly, we banter and tease,
In midnight's fun, there's nothing to please.
So snuggle up close, let those giggles flow,
For joy in the night is the best kind of glow.

Shades of Softness Unfolding

Softness lies waiting, a playful delight,
In every fold, a giggle takes flight.
Hiding in cushions, a leap and a roll,
A tapestry woven to humor the soul.

With shades of laughter, the night does enfold,
Each whisper a secret, a story retold.
On fluffy clouds of marshmallow cheer,
Even the shadows can't help but draw near.

Cuddly companions join in with glee,
As the fabric enchants with its jubilee spree.
Layers of joy in a midnight spree,
A comedy show nestled in quilted decree.

So roll in the laughter, unfold the delight,
For in the softness, the world seems just right.
As colors combine in the dark blue hue,
We dance with shadows, there's much more to do.

Feathered Touches of Serenity

To feathered whispers, the night takes form,
Where chuckles flutter, in every norm.
A pillow fight starts, with a giggly swoosh,
Serenity dances, all shaken and whoosh!

Under the starlight, the feathery fun,
A ruckus of joy, oh, but no one's done!
It tickles the toes and brushes the chin,
In this lighthearted night, we all dive in.

With laughter cascading like a gentle tease,
Every touch feels like a playful breeze.
In tiny moments, we find such delight,
Feathers of joy swirl, painting the night.

So snuggle in deeper, let giggles abound,
For in the soft chaos, true peace can be found.
With feathered touches, we lighten the mood,
And in the embrace of laughter, we're glued.

The Comfort of Softened Graces

A couch that hugs like mom's embrace,
Its cushions giggle, make me race.
With popcorn scattered, I take a leap,
This cozy throne makes me lose sleep.

The blanket's here, a hefty hug,
It swallows me, the warmth, a drug.
The sofa grins with every snack,
I wave goodbye to six-pack flack.

Each fiber whispers tales of joy,
Like cheeky rogues, they're here to toy.
In this snug realm, I rule with glee,
A soft kingdom, come share with me!

So raise a cheer for every pillowed whim,
For laughter flows when comforts brim.
In this realm, where coziness reigns,
Life's too short to feel those chains.

Grains of Silk Underfoot

A mishap happens on this silky road,
I slip and spin, oh how I glowed.
The floor beneath, a slippery muse,
In a dance I never meant to choose.

With every step, a comedy show,
I strut and slide like I am pro.
An unseen force beneath my feet,
This floor's a stage for my defeat.

I swear this rug has slipped my mind,
It laughs aloud, so unrefined.
But oh, the thrill of each wild twirl,
It turns my frown into a whirl.

So let us dance on grains of silk,
With skills akin to that of milk.
For every fall, a giggle bursts,
In laughter's tide, my heart it thirsts.

The Sweet Embrace of Dusk

As twilight spreads its sleepy arms,
The stars pop out with graceful charms.
The moon deems us a funny sight,
In shadows dancing, what pure delight.

With mugs of cocoa, we spill our cheer,
The cozy vibes are oh so near.
Each sip a giggle, a whimsical dream,
In dusky light, our laughter beams.

The fire crackles, a comedic show,
With marshmallows dancing, look at them go!
In this dim warmth, jokes take flight,
As dreamers join in the silky night.

So gather round, all hearts and souls,
In dusk's embrace, we play our roles.
With every chuckle, a tale unfurls,
Amidst the glow, joy swirls and twirls.

Graceful Shadows of a Woven Embrace

In this tapestry of light and shade,
Shadows dance with a funny parade.
Each thread a giggle, woven with grace,
They trip and tumble, a raucous race.

The fabric quivers with every joke,
As whispers spin, the laughter woke.
In cozy corners, we sit aligned,
With clever quips, hilarity combined.

Look at those shadows, mischief they sow,
With giddy grins, they steal the show.
A woven hug that holds us tight,
In playful banter, we find the light.

So let the shadows lead the way,
In every twist, let laughter play.
For in this dance of woven delight,
The joy springs forth, both day and night.

Draped in Layers of Dreams

With layers thick, I roam about,
Like a burrito, full of clout.
Dreams wrapped tight in fabric flair,
Can't find my feet, they're in midair!

This cloak of fabric pulls me in,
Dancing like a fool, I grin.
My kitten thinks it's all a game,
She pounces hard - oh, what a shame!

I trip on seams, fall on my back,
Like a pancake, there's no lack.
Laughter bubbles, fills the space,
In this fabric, I find my grace.

So here I am, a sight to see,
A cozy quilt, that's just on me.
With every twist and every spin,
I'm draped in dreams, let the fun begin!

Moonlight on a Silken Path

Underneath the silver glow,
Slipping on this sheet, oh no!
Moonlight guides my silly dance,
I trip again, can't miss my chance.

Silk beneath my flailing feet,
Wobbling like a wobbly beet.
The stars above are laughing loud,
While I bumble, oh, so proud!

A path so smooth, it leads me on,
My balletic skills all gone.
With each misstep, the giggles grow,
As I swirl and twist below.

So here I waltz on starlit seams,
Crafting magic from my dreams.
Each stumble's just a part of fun,
With laughter shared, we all have won!

Threads of Elysian Comfort

Wrapped in threads of soft delight,
I look divine, a silly sight.
Couches call, I start to blend,
As cushions tease, my time to spend.

I feel like royalty, oh dear!
A throne at home, it's quite unclear.
My dog is snoring, missing out,
While I perform this fabric route.

Each thread a whisper, soft and sweet,
But my laundry basket's my defeat.
Falling gently, a fabric heap,
I dream while laying in my sleep.

With each fluff and playful spin,
I'm diving back where fun begins.
Cozy chaos, oh, what a champ,
In threads so plush, I set the lamp!

Hushed Echoes of Velvet Nights

In velvet nights, I prance and play,
Whispers giggle in their sway.
Owls burst out in laughter bright,
As I tumble, what a sight!

The moon beams down, a soft embrace,
While I trip through this charming space.
Echoes murmur, soft and light,
As I roll around with all my might.

Each ruffle wraps me in delight,
A clownish dance, oh, what a fright!
With every laugh, I prance anew,
In velvet lanes, it's quite the zoo!

The night goes on, the fun runs deep,
In hushed echoes, dreams I keep.
With velvet hugs and laughter's call,
I stumble forth, embracing all!

Hushed Murmurs of Lush Textures

In shadows soft, a gentle tease,
A fabric's whisper floats with ease.
It tickles toes and laughs a tune,
Bringing joy like a playful moon.

A couch that winks, a throw that sighs,
Secret giggles where comfort lies.
Cuddle up, ignore the mess,
As cozy dreams earn their success.

With every fold, a story spins,
Of daring cats and slapstick wins.
A tumble here, a roll over there,
Laughter brightens the velvet air.

So let us lounge, and let us play,
In fuzzy bliss, we'll drift away.
With soft fondness, life's a jest,
In textures lush, we find our rest.

The Cloak of Night's Enchantment

Under a cover of starry dreams,
A cloak that tickles – or so it seems.
Whispers of twinkles dance all around,
While mischief lurks without a sound.

Each twirl of darkness, a playful jest,
As shadows join in a silent quest.
Laughter hid beneath shimmering hues,
In midnight's pranks, what fun ensues!

The moon beams bright, a giggle or two,
A dash of whimsy in every view.
With sparkling smiles and midnight glee,
We relish the night's unpredictability.

So let's embrace this velvet sphere,
With chuckles and thrills, we have no fear.
Night's enchantment, pure delight,
Wraps us warmly till morning light.

Embracing the Warmth of Dreams

Snug in blankets, we start to drift,
Infused with laughter, a playful gift.
Pillow fights and giggles abound,
In cozy realms where joy is found.

Each dream a tapestry, bright and bold,
With tales of mischief and secrets told.
As snuggly duvets wrap us tight,
We dance through fun even in the night.

In whimsy's grip, we float away,
To lands where silliness holds sway.
The world outside may wear a frown,
But here, we wear our laughter crown.

So cuddle close, let worries cease,
In the warmth of dreams, we find our peace.
A quilt of joy, oh what a theme,
As we embrace the night's sweet whimsy.

Tender Silhouettes of Dusk

As twilight sprawls, the day grows shy,
With silly shadows that frolic by.
They stretch and bend, a playful sight,
In hues of laughter, soft and bright.

The sun dips low; the giggles rise,
With twilight hues, a grand surprise.
Each silhouette whispers a secret tune,
Daring us to join their little swoon.

The night reveals a mischievous plot,
As hours giggle away the thought.
Tender hues brush the playful sky,
In faded light where chuckles lie.

So let us dance in dusk's embrace,
With joyous whispers, we'll find our place.
In tender silhouettes, we'll play along,
With laughter's echo, our hearts belong.

Lush Embraces of an Autumn Night

Beneath the stars, we dance and sway,
In jackets too snug, we laugh and play.
With each little bump, we trip and shout,
The leaves just chuckle, while we spin about.

The moon's a joker, shining so bright,
It lights our paths on this comical night.
With grand missteps and wild twirls,
We swirl through the air, like laughing squirrels.

Laughter echoes under the trees,
As nature sings soft lilting pleas.
A fabulous mess, we couldn't care less,
The autumn's embrace, a silly, warm dress.

And when we fall flat into the leaves,
The crunching sound sends us into heaves.
Wrapped up in giggles, the world feels right,
In lush embraces of an autumn night.

Secrets Heartfelt and Soft

A whisper of joy in the morning sun,
Trapped in my pocket, a giggle on the run.
Secretive nudges, a playful poke,
A tickle of laughter from the ticklish oak.

With jokes that flutter like leaves in the breeze,
We share our thoughts, like flowers with bees.
Nonsense blooms in every crack,
The humor spills forth, no need to hold back.

In a world of giggles, we trace silly lines,
Doodles and wishes tangled with vines.
Heartfelt secrets in the softest of tones,
Spreading like warmth, in our happy zones.

With friends by our side, we flourish and spin,
Our laughter, the drum, inviting a grin.
In whispered delight, we revel as we talk,
Guardians of giggles, on this soft, sunny walk.

Soft Petals in a Silver Mist

Morning dew sparkles, all silly and bright,
Hiding behind petals, what a funny sight!
They giggle and sway in the chill of the dawn,
Wearing their freshness like a giddy fawn.

Each bloom whispers jokes to the wandering breeze,
While butterflies laugh, doing loops with such ease.
Nature's comedy act, unfolding at dawn,
A bouquet of chuckles on the soft, lush lawn.

With petals that tease and tickle our toes,
We prance through the garden, ignoring our woes.
Silver mist giggles, weaving in and out,
Crafting a chorus of joyous shout.

In this floral theater, we all play a part,
A scene filled with laughter, tucked in the heart.
Soft petals in laughter, they sway and they twist,
What a delightful way to live, laughed and kissed!

A Gentle Tide of Comfort

In the embrace of waves, we float and glide,
A gentle tide that pulls us inside.
With shrieks of delight, we splash all around,
Our joyful chaos, a musical sound.

Waves tumble and dance like clowns in a show,
Each swell a whisper, each churn a funny flow.
With sand in our toes, we giggle and play,
The tide of comfort sweeps stress away.

As seaweed tickles, we tumble and roll,
The ocean's a joker, with humor to stroll.
In the surface's shimmer, we find our sweet laugh,
Chasing away worries, slicing the path.

So here we will splash, till the stars fill the sky,
In the glow of the moon, our spirits fly high.
A gentle tide brings joy, and oh what a show,
In our sandy escapades, we flourish and grow.

The Luxuriant Glow of Dusk

As dusk descends, a silly sight,
A cat in a coat too snug and tight.
It struts like a model, full of glee,
Blind to how funny that coat can be.

The leaves start to whisper, the trees have a chat,
While squirrels wear capes—imagine that!
They slide down the branches, with flair and with pride,
In this soft, glowing light, let's all take a ride.

The shadows stretch long, the sky turns to peach,
A dog tries to dance, at the end of the beach.
With paws in the air and a wagging tail,
It trips on its leash but won't let it fail.

So let's toast to the dusk, so rich and so bold,
With a wink to the night—it's a sight to behold!
In playful abandon, the world feels light,
As laughter and whimsy fill up the night.

A Symphony of Gentle Sensations

The tickle of feathers, the fluffs of delight,
As a goose in a tutu takes off in flight.
With music of giggles, it prances away,
Making sure all the cows join in the play.

A bubbly balloon floats past a neat fence,
It dances with daisies—what perfect suspense!
The colors blend softly, a pastel parade,
Creating a symphony, jovial and frayed.

With cupcakes on chairs and sprinkles on hats,
A marching band forms with a bunch of fat cats.
They sway to the rhythm, each one wears a grin,
As joy takes the stage—let the madness begin!

So let's twirl in our jammies, with popcorn in hand,
As laughter erupts from this soft, wondrous land.
A festival of silliness under the moon,
Where fun reigns supreme, and the heart's the grand tune.

The Dance of Softness

In a meadow of fluff, where giggles abound,
A bunny's perplexed by a lost, fluffy sound.
It hops in small circles, then leaps with a flair,
Wearing mismatched socks—it's a sight rare to share.

The fireflies twinkle, they lead the parade,
With ants on a mission, all set to invade.
They march to the rhythm of a grasshopper's song,
In this dance of soft wonders, where no one feels wrong.

A hedgehog in slippers, so cozy and round,
Decides to join in, but oh, what a sound!
With each little shuffle, it gently rolls 'round,
Creating a laughter that echoes the ground.

So gather your giggles, and sway with the breeze,
As the fluffy creatures dance with ultimate ease.
In this whimsical soft world, laughter will grow,
A joyful ballet where the heart's in the show.

Where Velvet Shadows Reside

In a land where the shadows are fluffy and round,
An owl in pajamas flies off the ground.
It hoots a delight with a wink in its eye,
While rabbits in formation just giggle and sigh.

Underneath the starlight, the fireflies race,
In glittery costumes, they brighten the space.
The crickets are chirping a soft lullaby,
And the playfully lost—oh, they just can't fly.

A fox with a top hat prances in glee,
It's quite the odd ball, but who's there to see?
With a tap and a twirl in the moonlight's embrace,
The creatures conspire to set quite the pace.

So join in the fun, where the shadows reside,
In this silly realm, let your worries slide.
With laughter as currency, joy as the prize,
We'll play in this velvet-tinged paradise.

Velvet Whispers in the Dark

In shadows soft, a giggle rings,
A couch that laughs and blanket sings,
The moonlight's touch, it gives a wink,
A playful dance on the brink.

A cat in capes, prances about,
In secret games, they flit and shout,
With every scratch, the purring flows,
As laughter fills the night that glows.

A hidden stash of snacks nearby,
Whispers of crumbs that softly sigh,
Tickling tales in the midnight air,
As friends unite, with naught a care.

So here's to nights with soft delight,
Where fuzzy dreams take playful flight,
With velvet whispers, hearts embark,
On silly journeys 'neath the dark.

Gossamer Hands of Twilight

As twilight wraps the world so bright,
A giggle sneaks into the night,
With fingers light, they tease and play,
And chase the stars that won't delay.

In tulle adorned, the fairies spin,
A dance of dusk where laughs begin,
With gossamer gloves, they poke and prod,
While all the while, they wink at God.

The moon, a grin, sends shadows wide,
As playful spirits come to slide,
The night's a stage for mirth and jest,
With cotton candy dreams, we rest.

With every sigh, a melody,
Of whispered winds, oh can't you see?
Twilight's hands rustle, wrap, and twirl,
In a world alive, where laughter swirls.

Silken Threads of Memory

A tapestry made from giggles bright,
In afternoons that slip from sight,
With every thread, a tale goes round,
A patch of joy, forever found.

From silly hats to socks that chirp,
In vibrant hues, they twist and burp,
Knots of laughter intertwine fast,
Oh memories made, they always last!

Through silken strands, the stories weave,
In every knot, we can believe,
A bouncy bounce, a wiggle there,
As threads of joy fill every chair.

So here's a sock, a whimsical gift,
In memory's glow, our spirits lift,
With silken threads, our laughter binds,
In crazy patterns life unwinds.

Mossy Hues and Gentle Tones

In mossy shades, the laughter grows,
As giggly sprites in soft light pose,
With hues of green and blushy pink,
They share a wink, no need to think.

A spongey step, they leap and bound,
In gentle tones, their joy is found,
With every hop, a chuckle springs,
In nature's arms, the mischief sings.

With playful jests in every leaf,
They weave a tapestry of relief,
In shades just right, they whisper low,
Of silly things we used to know.

So come and join this frolicking,
With mossy hues as bellies sting,
In gentle tones, we'll skip along,
With laughter echoed in our song.

In the Heart of Tenderness

In the softest nook of the room,
Lies a cat in its feathery plume.
It thinks it's a king on a throne,
Only to awaken, still all alone.

A neighbor's dog, with a wagging tail,
Snores like a train on a great big trail.
In dreams of peanut butter galore,
He dances on clouds, who could ask for more?

A warm blanket drapes like a hug,
But catches your foot like a sly little bug.
You trip and you tumble, oh dear, oh no!
A giggle erupts, that sweet, silly show.

Laughter bounces off walls so round,
In this funny refuge, joy is found.
With a hint of mischief and much to share,
We savor the moments light as air.

Threads that Bind in Warm Embrace.

A sweater two sizes too big, oh my!
It swallows me whole, should I laugh or cry?
I wear it proudly, like a cozy sack,
A fashion statement, or a wardrobe hack?

The yarn unraveled from Grandma's sock,
Entangled my feet like a bad prank clock.
I dance with the threads, a wild ballet,
Only to trip, in a comedic display.

Quilts made of memories, soft as can be,
They whisper the tales of my family tree.
Each patch a story, with smiles and tears,
A patchwork of laughter through all of the years.

In this warm embrace, I roll on the floor,
With pillows that cushion my playful uproar.
So here's to the knitters, the seamsters so grand,
For binding us closer, with stitches so planned.

Whispers of Silken Dreams

A pair of slippers that squeak when I walk,
Echo my thoughts like a chatty old clock.
They're soft and inviting, yet clumsy to wear,
I tiptoe in giggles, sloshed without care.

A scarf wrapped too tight, in a great wool embrace,
Feels like a hug from a grandma's warm face.
Yet, when I attempt to flaunt my great style,
I choke and I wheeze – oh, it's been a while!

Beneath silken sheets where my dreams go to play,
I've battled with pillows in a feathery fray.
Each toss and each turn, a giggle-filled spree,
As I wrestle with comfort, who's winning? Not me!

The laughter erupts with a snicker and sigh,
As I roll off the bed, how did I fly?
In silken dreams, with a giggle so grand,
What fun we find in this whimsical land.

In the Embrace of Soft Shadows

The curtains sway gently, tickled by breeze,
They catch dust bunnies, oh what a tease!
In the corners, they dance like mischievous sprites,
Craving a swan song beneath the moonlight.

A lamp with a shade that tilts just askew,
Projects funny shapes - look, a dog in a shoe!
As I chuckle at shadows that play on the floor,
I think of the chaos my house can't ignore.

In plush little chairs that swallow me whole,
I sink in the softness that bubbles my soul.
With whispers of stories from cushions around,
Soft laughter and warmth in this haven I've found.

These shadows, they giggle, and so do I,
In this cozy retreat, where silliness flies.
So here's to the embraces that lighten our loads,
With tickles and chuckles along life's great roads.

A Gentle Humming in the Dark

In the night, a silly tune,
A cat in socks, dancing soon.
With every step, the floor does squeak,
A velvet vibe, oh what a freak!

The moonlight glints on chips of cheese,
As mice hold disco, if you please.
A party thrown by those who creep,
In shadows where the giggles leap.

Elbow in a bowl of cream,
A furry friend joins in the dream.
Together twirling, paws in flight,
In a dark room, a silly sight!

With laughter echoing off the walls,
A gentle hum in twilight calls.
The rhythm of the night unfolds,
As secrets in the shadows scold.

The Pull of Mellow Elegance

A snail on a tie walks in style,
With fancy shoes, he stamps and smiles.
A velvet cap, perched on his head,
He glides through puddles, quite well-fed.

Dancing ants with top hats flair,
Turn table spins, oh what a pair!
With every twirl, they knock the snacks,
In velvet puffs, they've got no lacks.

A ladybug joins in the quirk,
They shimmy, shake, and wildly jerk.
With every misstep, giggles burst,
In the charm of chaos, they'll quench their thirst.

Mellow colors swirl and play,
As laughter wraps the night away.
In elegance of funny tones,
They disco dance on mushroom thrones.

Where Softness Meets Dreams

In a world where fluff comes alive,
Bouncing pillows begin to thrive.
They gather 'round for pillow fights,
A fluffy fun that spins all nights.

Dreams ride in on cotton clouds,
While ducklings quack in cheerful crowds.
With sleepy eyes and cozy cheer,
The soft embraces banish fear.

A teddy bear trips on a shoe,
He giggles out loud, what else is new?
In this land of fluffy delight,
Where dreams and laughter twirl in flight.

As daybreak peeks, the giggles fade,
Yet softness lingers, never strayed.
With echoes of fun tucked away,
Until the next fluffy play-day!

Threads of Comfort in Twilight

At twilight's gate, a sweater knits,
A ghost slips on, then starts to sit.
With every stitch, he tells a jest,
A knitted laugh, he loves the best.

The yarn unwinds with silly grace,
As puns and patterns intertwine in space.
A cozy web of giggles spun,
Each twisted loop, a funny pun.

A dancing loom with fabric dreams,
With threads of joy, nothing's as it seems.
The twilight whispers silk and fun,
As laughter weaves 'til day is done.

In the quiet hum of evening's song,
Comfort reigns where the silly belong.
Threads of warmth, where giggles dwell,
In twilight's arms, all is well!

Embraced by the Fabric of Dawn

In the morning's gentle light,
A cat finds a blanket to bite,
With claws that dance and prance,
He's now in a fuzzy romance.

As sunlight spills, all sleek and bright,
He lounges like a king in flight,
With purring tunes, he starts to play,
A comedy at the dawn of day.

The fabric wraps him close and tight,
Engaging in a morning fight,
With shadows tossed and blankets stirred,
He's the fluffiest knight, undeterred.

Through laughter shared with fabric fine,
He dreams of mice and endless time,
In a world where soft things are fun,
His day begins; the game's just begun.

Softly Woven Secrets

In a world of fluff and fluffier dreams,
A squirrel plots, or so it seems,
With secret stash of every thread,
He knits a hat for his dear head.

With needles made from shiny sticks,
He stitches fast, with funny tricks,
His pals all gather round to peek,
At the hiccuping squirrel's technique.

Each loop a giggle, every yarn a cheer,
Their laughter waves, it casts a sphere,
Of joy that wraps around so tight,
In woven secrets, pure delight.

And when the hat is tried at last,
It tumbles down, oh, what a blast!
For squirrels, hats are but a game,
Yet every stitch earns squirrel fame!

Veils of Softest Surrender

A dog in blankets takes a stand,
Believing he's the finest band,
With every wag, a fabric sway,
He leads a parade of fluff today.

His buddies join, the feline crew,
In silky veils of purple hue,
They twirl and leap, like stars at night,
In comedy, they find their flight.

As laughter floats, they spin around,
In tangled frames, they're tightly bound,
Each purr and bark, a joyous song,
In softest layers where they belong.

With fabric dreams, they softly play,
A frolic through the light of day,
In veils of laughter, they can't resist,
A funny tale, they can't dismiss.

Slumbering Under a Silken Sky

A pig in pajamas snores away,
In cozy dreams, he dreams of hay,
His snores are like a lullaby,
To cows who dance and leap nearby.

Under skies of pastel sheets,
The barnyard sings to funny beats,
As chickens chuckle in delight,
And roosters strut without a fright.

With every flutter, every chirp,
They wake him up with a little jerk,
Yet underneath that silky quilt,
He grins and laughs, his dreams won't wilt.

A slumber party in the barn,
Where laughter echoes, none can harm,
In softest fabrics, joy abounds,
Where sleepy giggles know no bounds.

Silken Reverie of Grace

A cat on a rug, so snug, so wise,
Dreams of fish in the skies.
With paws tucked in, it sneaks a pounce,
Chasing shadows, what a bounce!

In the afternoon glow, our couch makes a scene,
As my dog munches chips, paws shiny and clean.
What a sight, my furry friend,
In a snack-attack fury, no accident to mend!

The curtains dance slowly, a breeze with a twist,
While I trip on my foot, oh, how could I miss?
Laughter erupts, my face goes all red,
As the parakeet snickers and bobs its bright head!

A plush little pillow holds giggles of cheer,
As we lounge in our paradise, heaven is near.
Between chuckles and snorts, we bask in delight,
In our silken world, everything feels just right.

Gentle Affections in Twilight

Under cushions, I seek my lost phone,
But find crumbs of cookies, now fully blown.
The kids giggle, pointing at fur on my sleeve,
While our cat does a dance, oh, what a weave!

Twilight kisses the room with blushes and jokes,
As we sip on warm cocoa and tell tales of folks.
Each story a legend, with laughter through tears,
Puffing like marshmallows; oh, how time cheers!

The dog tilts his head, like he's heard it all,
His tail wagging wild, passing no judgment at all.
With a belly full of giggles, we sink to the floor,
In our plush paradise, who could want more?

A soft cuddle pile—best therapy yet,
With pillows that giggle—what a friendly set!
Tonight, we're wrapped in warmth and delight,
As the moon winks at our cozy, fun night.

Emotions Wrapped in Ease

In the comfort of chaos, we find such joy,
As I dodge the cat's leap with a well-timed ploy.
Mom laughs so hard, she spills her sweet tea,
While dad sneezes loudly, like an old bumblebee!

Cushions become forts, the couch breathes with cheer,
A kingdom of laughter, our royal frontier.
With a tap on the head, like a gentle goodbye,
The ginger cat reigns, with a watchful eye!

Tickle fights are fierce, laughter erupts,
As the dog joins the fray, with playful yips and jumps.
His tail wags like a flag, a banner of glee,
In a world of snug pillows, my favorite spree!

As we snuggle quite close, filled with whimsy and fun,
Jokes bounce around like a duck on the run.
Oh, what a night, with each hug and tease,
Wrapped in our warmth, we find perfect ease.

Sway of Softness Beneath Stars

Beneath the vast heavens, our blanket unfolds,
As we share silly stories, both bold and retold.
Our laughter a melody, floating through night,
While the stars twinkle back, what a sight!

The dog snores softly, a tune so surreal,
As I tell him my dreams with the utmost appeal.
The moon gives a chuckle, drip-dripping its light,
On our cozy gathering, oh, what a night!

Pillows in chaos, we wiggle around,
In a whimsical world, where giggles abound.
With faces that shine like bright shooting stars,
While we roll in the grass, forgetting our scars!

So let's dance through the evening, till eyelids do close,
In a velvety canvas, where happiness grows.
With stars as our witnesses, let's cherish this spree,
For the softness of laughter is the best remedy.

Among the Clouds of Warmth

In a world where socks don't match,
And coffee spills on shirts we snatch,
We float on clouds of fluffy cheer,
Laughing boisterously, never fear.

A gentle poke, a silly tease,
Feathered pillows, if you please,
We bounce like kids, in clumsy glee,
Chasing dreams wildly, as we flee.

With goofy grins and snickers loud,
We dance around, feeling quite proud,
Our joy's the sun on chilly days,
Spreading warmth in quirky ways.

So if you trip, just take a bow,
Embrace the fall, oh, here and now,
For in this warmth, we find our way,
And laugh through life, come what may.

The Embrace of Gentle Feathers

A tickle here, a nudge right there,
Feathers floating through the air,
With every poke, a playful shove,
We giggle tight; oh, how we love!

Whimsical hats, mismatched shoes,
In this light, we shake off blues,
We roll and tumble, soft delight,
Under fluffy clouds, we take flight.

Bouncing pillows all around,
In a hub of laughter, we are bound,
With feathered friends to see us through,
Life's just a game with this silly crew.

So let us dance, as shadows flee,
In this embrace, just you and me,
Funny stories sprinkled bright,
Feathers and laughter day and night.

A Tapestry of Comforted Souls

In a room where chaos reigns supreme,
We gather close, we plot and scheme,
Stitching tales with threads of fun,
Twisting yarns 'til the day is done.

We weave together laughter's song,
In a tapestry that feels so wrong,
Mismatched colors, yet so divine,
Crafting memories on a crooked line.

With comical quirks and silly grins,
The best of laughter, that's how it begins,
In knots and loops, we twine our fate,
Finding joy in the words we create.

So here we sit, side by side,
In this patchwork, we hold our pride,
For within these threads of bonding light,
Our comfort grows, shining bright.

Silken Caress of Dawn

Morning rays with a silly grin,
Awakening chaos, where to begin?
Bright pajamas, funky and loud,
We dance through breakfast, oh, how we're proud!

With spoons like trumpets, we take a stand,
Syrup rivers, pancakes so grand,
Flipping flapjacks, a comical flight,
As laughter spills into morning light.

We twirl around like dainty swans,
Wearing smiles in our sleep-deprived yawns,
In this silken caress, we find our way,
Chasing sleepy blues to keep at bay.

So raise your cups, let's toast our dawn,
To silly tales until they're gone,
With giggles warm, and hearts so bright,
We embrace the day, with pure delight.

In the Lushness of Nightfall

A bunny prances, out on a spree,
Dressed in plush, so fancy and free.
He thinks he's suave, a real true gent,
But trips on a leaf, oh what a event!

Stars twinkle, as if they conspire,
While he hums along to his own choir.
His fluffy tail sways, a sight to behold,
He can't quite decide if he's brave or bold.

Nearby, a cat with a touch of sass,
Watches him trip, then starts to laugh.
"Oh darling bunny, what's the rush?"
"Do you think that makes you look like a plush?"

So the night carries on with giggles and cheer,
As critters prance under skies bright and clear.
With velvet-like dreams weaving through the air,
In the lushness of nightfall, there's always a flair.

The Allure of Silken Nights

A silk-wrapped squirrel, oh what a sight,
Strutting his stuff in the pale moonlight.
He's dressed to impress, with a style so grand,
But trips on his scarf, oh isn't that bland?

The owls are hooting, sharing the fun,
As the dandy squirrel tries to outrun.
He twirls and he spins, in a silky ballet,
Until he gets dizzy, and fades away.

A feathery chicken, with feathers so bright,
Quips, "Hey, Mr. Squirrel, keep it upright!"
With a playful wink, she struts and clucks,
While our beloved hero is stuck in the muck.

Yet the charm of the night won't let him stay down,
He hops to his feet, adjusts his fine gown.
With laughter and joy in the whimsical night,
The allure of silken nights is pure delight!

Delicate Echoes in Moonlight

A mouse in a tux makes a comical dash,
He's late to a party, his cheeks in a flash.
He skitters and squeaks, like a tiny madman,
With dreams of cheese, he's got quite a plan!

Yet as he arrives, trip over a shoe,
Falls right in front of the guests, oh boo hoo!
The crowd erupts in a cacophony of glee,
While he picks himself up, quite gracefully.

With moonlight casting delicate shadows,
He shakes off the dust from his fancy toes.
"Fear not, dear friends, I'm here for the spread!"
As trays of snacks dance in his hungry head.

So the night goes on, filled with zest and cheer,
With echoes of laughter, crystal clear.
In delicate whispers beneath silvery beams,
He nibbles and dances, all fueled by his dreams.

Gentle Textures of Desire

A fluffy dog sporting a snazzy bow tie,
Struts through the park as the birds fly by.
The ladies all swoon, "Oh, what a charmer!"
But he leaps in a puddle, looking much less calmer!

With mud on his coat and a blank little stare,
He shakes off the mess, as if not a care.
"Who needs a bath when you've got a good time?"
He wags his tail, thinking he's in his prime.

Nearby, a prancing cat rolls her eyes,
"Is that your best look? I can't disguise!"
Yet even through jest, they share a bright bond,
In the gentle textures, their friendship grows strong.

So as the sun sets on that playful spree,
Everyone knows it's best to be free.
With scruffy charm and the sauces of life,
Joy swells in laughter, cutting through strife.

Delicate Hues of Dusk

A cat in a coat, so sleek and so sly,
Chasing shadows that dance, oh me, oh my!
With paws dipped in twilight, it's quite the sight,
As giggles escape in the fading light.

The sky's painted purple, a cheeky little grin,
While the moon hides behind, thinking it's kin.
Stars twinkle in laughter, a cosmic jest,
While I trip on my laces, the universe blessed.

A flight of bold swallows, all flap and no aim,
Crashing into each other, but nobody's to blame.
In this fun twilight hour, so whimsically steep,
I laugh at the chaos, from slumber, I creep.

With delights in the air, like sugar on toast,
I reckon the sunset deserves a grand boast.
In hues oh so gentle, fade to that night,
Where giggles abound, and all feels just right.

The Caress of Evening's Cloak

Now dusk wraps around, with fingers of glee,
Turning my garden to comedy, whee!
A bumblebee stumbles right into a rose,
With petals like curtains, it strikes a pose.

The dog in a bowtie, oh what a sight!
He winks at the moon like it's all very light.
The crickets hold concerts, just out of tune,
As I bop to their tune under a big yellow moon.

With pockets of laughter, the night takes the stage,
Where the stars spin their tales, inked on a page.
As the air turns to laughter, so rich and ornate,
I dance with the shadows, what a funny fate!

The night will not end, it's a never-ending jest,
Every whisper of wind is a giggle expressed.
Wrapped snug in the twilight, a cozy embrace,
Where the fun never stops, it's a curious place.

Hidden Depths of Softness

In a pile of cushions, I dive and I sink,
Where softness surrounds, and I giggle, I think.
The cat pounces in, on the quest for a nap,
But pounces right out with a flustered flap!

The couch becomes lava, I must navigate,
With pillows like boats, I won't hesitate.
Each step is a laugh, a soft, squishy tide,
In this sea of plush wonders, I slide and I glide.

Alarms like squirrels scurry, and chuckles arise,
When the remote goes missing, oh what a surprise!
The search leads to treasures, both odd and quite nice,
Like snacks from last week – who ordered this spice?

Nestled in fluff, all worries take flight,
As echoes of laughter fill up the night.
In hidden soft depths, where humor is keen,
I find joy submerged in a world oh-so-sheen.

Luxurious Echoes of Touch

Oh, the plushness of life, it drapes and it sways,
While I chase through the laughter, what a tangled maze!
The sofa's an island, I'm the king of the fluff,
With pillows my subjects, it's definitely enough!

In velvety dreams where the giggles all start,
The cat plays the harp, with a flick of his heart.
While slippers conspire to trip me once more,
Each step is an echo that leaves me in sore.

The rug plays the host to a bouncing parade,
As dust bunnies cheer for the antics repaid.
With laughter like bubbles that light up the room,
I dance with the echoes, till they burst with a boom!

When twilight arrives on its soft, cozy train,
I snuggle with memories, oh what a gain!
With luxurious whispers, the night takes its hold,
And in the warm velvet of laughter, I'm bold.

Cradle of Cashmere Nights

In the depths of evening light,
A cozy seat, so soft and right,
With cushions plumped and blankets near,
I laugh and sigh without a fear.

Snuggled up in threads of glee,
Where every fiber speaks to me,
I nod to cats who stroll around,
In cashmere realms, all joy is found.

The chair squeaks loud, a funny song,
As I declare, I don't belong,
Yet here I stay, 'neath evening's glow,
In cuddly dreams, we steal the show.

With every brush against my skin,
The laughter twirls, the joy begins,
A cradle soft, with giggles spun,
These cashmere nights are purest fun!

The Sigh of Soft Fabrics

When I wrap up in all things plush,
My silly brain begins to mush,
A fluffy robe, I cannot take,
With pockets deep, I'm wide awake.

Each time I plop, I hear a squeak,
A symphony of laughs I seek,
These gentle threads, they tease and play,
In my soft castle, I'll laugh today.

I drape myself like playful dough,
With patterns swirled, just like a show,
The fabrics dance, they wrap, they twist,
In silky joy, you can't resist.

So join me now, let's fluff and fold,
In cotton clouds, where warmth is gold,
We'll laugh until our faces ache,
In soft embrace, for humor's sake!

Woven Whispers of Comfort

In threads of laughter, we entwine,
With every stitch, our joy aligns,
The whispers soft, they tease the air,
A tapestry of fun to share.

In every nook, a tale is spun,
Where Cozy Joe has just begun,
To crack a joke, to stretch and play,
In woven warmth, we chuckle away.

Patched together, quirks unfold,
With panels soft, and seams of gold,
We gather close, a merry band,
To weave the dreams that life has planned.

So grab a pillow, don't be shy,
In woven arms, let laughter fly,
With every hug, the fibers sing,
In whispered joys, we find our spring!

Vital Threads of Serenity

In the chaos, I seek a space,
Where laughter meets a cozy face,
With threads that wrap like warm delight,
I giggle softly through the night.

Each stitch a cause for silly cheer,
In cuddly fabrics, truth is clear,
With gentle hugs, I toast the breeze,
And dance about with such great ease.

The patterns clash, a funny sight,
With polka dots and stripes so bright,
I tumble forth in soft ballet,
Draped in joy, I twirl and sway.

So come, my friends, let's find a chair,
In threads of humor, none compare,
With every smile, we calm the storm,
In our snug world, we feel so warm!

www.ingramcontent.com/pod-product-compliance
Lightning Source LLC
Chambersburg PA
CBHW060135230426
43661CB00003B/425